Writing

Police

Reports

A *Practical* Guide

Alec Ross
David Plant

Motorola Teleprograms, Inc., 4825 N. Scott St., Suite 23, Schiller Park, Ill. 60176

Table of Contents

Every Book Should Have An Introduction.

This Is It.

You can be taught to be a welder, a nurse, a brain surgeon, a safe cracker, or a police officer. But you *can't* be taught to be a creative writer.

You can not be taught to be a poet, an architect, a fashion designer, or an actor. But you *can* be taught to be a report writer.

In other words, you can be taught a technique, but you can't be taught to be an artist. Some personal, individual quality of your own has to be merged with a learned technique in order for an artist to be created. Philosophers have spent centuries trying to understand and to explain this process. Fortunately, for our immediate purpose, we can leave them to their labors; we are concerned with only a technique, not an art.

The technique of reporting is one that can be

learned by anyone who possesses two basic qualities: fundamental communication skills and a trained ability to observe. You already have a start on both of these qualities. If you didn't, you wouldn't be where you are right now, reading this book and saying to yourself something that sounds like this: "Oh my God, here we go again. I hate English, I have always hated English, and I always will hate English. I want to be a cop, so what the hell do I have to be a writer for?"

Don't worry. You are going to be a cop — or maybe you are one already — but you don't have to be a writer. Honest. Remember, you can't be taught to be a creative writer, so why should we all waste our time? For the purpose of this course, just forget that the word *writing* exists. Concentrate instead on the word *reporting*. For our purposes, the words can be interchanged, although you'll never convince an English teacher that the words mean the same thing. You are going to be a cop who knows how to make a report. Reporting goes with the territory; a cop who can't report is only half a cop.

Chapter 1

A Story That Could Have Happened

Officer Johnson's Report — Or Lack of It

Once upon a time, in a quiet little town, Officer Johnson was patrolling his regular beat. It wasn't the kind of town where very much happened ordinarily, but on that particular day Officer Johnson was very busy indeed.

First, he was on the scene of a collision in which an elderly couple was fatally injured. While waiting for the traffic detail and the ambulance help he had summoned, Johnson was able to be of some comfort to the dying couple.

Later in the day he stopped and, in general terms, warned a suspected juvenile bicycle thief that he had been keeping an eye on for some time.

He aided a mentally disturbed woman who

had wandered into the street from a nearby convalescent home. He had had some experience with this wanderer before, but fortunately he got her back to the home before she was hurt in traffic.

He also issued a warning to a man whose dog was busily digging up a complaining neighbor's prize azaleas, and, as usual, he allowed his presence to be seen right across the street from the main entrance of the high school at dismissal time. He didn't make a big deal out of this high school check, but he did nod and wave to some of his special student friends.

Good old Officer Johnson, always there when he was needed. He was familiar with his beat; he knew everyone and everyone knew him. Aside from the collision fatalities, it was just an ordinary, routine day, maybe a little busier than most, but nothing really special. And because there wasn't anything really special, Officer Johnson didn't write anything down. Traffic detail would write up the collision, but everything else was ordinary. Johnson always told people that he was a cop, not a damned pen pusher, and he had never been given any reason to change his mind about that. He couldn't be bothered with notebooks, citizen contact forms, complaint forms, field investigation reports, and all the rest of the junk that is being taught and demanded today. He took care of his beat his way, and really it was a very nice, comfortable day.

But then a whole series of unexpected things

started to happen, and Officer Johnson just wasn't ready.

The children and step-children of the dead couple became embroiled in a contest over their inheritance. Who had died first, the man or the woman? The decision would make a considerable difference to the potential heirs. There was no report available.

The parents of the suspected bicycle thief brought suit against the city, charging police harrassment of a minor, violation of civil rights, and assorted counts of racism and brutality. There was no report available.

The daughter of the disturbed and wandering patient moved her mother to another facility and refused to pay the billed charges of the convalescent home. The home sued for nonpayment and the daughter counter-sued for violation of a caretaking contract which she could prove by the officer's report. But no report was available.

The dog owner, following Johnson's instructions, tied his pet up, and the dog strangled to death on the rope. When the SPCA brought a charge of cruelty to animals against the owner, he said he was merely following police orders. No report of such orders was available.

The high school typing classroom was broken into that afternoon, and six expensive new typewriters were stolen. Four students were accused of the theft, but each argued that Officer Johnson had seen them leave school in a group that day. No report was available in

Johnson's notebook because Johnson didn't even have a notebook.

In each case, Officer Johnson was called as a witness. After all, he had been there at the start or the finish of each incident. All the parties involved remembered that he had been there, and it was only three months before the various cases got to court.

Guess what happened on the witness stand. You're right. Officer Johnson, with no notes or reports, could only approximate times and places. After all, every day was pretty much like every other. What he *thought* he remembered could not be accepted as evidence. Nothing was written down. Exactly what he had heard the dying couple say and in what order, exactly what words he used and what action he displayed toward the suspected bicycle thief, whether or not the disturbed patient was in immediate sight of the convalescent home attendants, whether or not he had specifically instructed the dog owner to *tie* up his pet, and exactly which students he saw leaving the high school — none of these vital facts could be established.

The lawsuits, trials, appeals seemed to go on forever. Nobody was really satisfied with their outcome. Some people lost a lot of money, some lost their liberty for a while, and everyone lost lots of time and reputation.

There's a different atmosphere on Officer Johnson's old beat now. The new officer isn't quite as friendly yet, but everyone is willing to give him time to meet people. He certainly seems busier than Johnson, always writing something down in his notebook. Nobody remembers Johnson ever doing anything like that, but then nobody really talks much about the old days on the beat. People haven't seen him in a long time, but wherever he is now, you can rest assured that nobody in town loves Officer Johnson anymore.

Now the story of Officer Johnson — which might very well be true — isn't designed to be a story about how to get the community to love a cop. It's nice to be loved, of course, but it's even nicer to do your job as well as it can possibly be done. Let love come as the result of achievement, not just of intention.

You decided to be a cop because you wanted to do things, and probably the first discovery you made was that as a cop you had to spend more time writing and less time doing. Seemingly everything you do has to be written down. Instead of doing all those exciting things that happen on television, you sit at a desk or in a patrol car or stand at a coffee counter and write down what you did and what you're doing, what you thought and what you're thinking. It's dull and you hate it and you don't do a very good job of it, and when you do get to the real stuff you have to interrupt it to write it all down. When do you get to be the kind of cop you wanted to be in the first place?

You don't.

You're going to go on doing what you're doing — writing what you're writing — for as long as you hold the job that you have. Get used to it. There's no escape. You're going to go on writing, turning out more words than any novelist, turning out more words each week than any English major could ever dream of. Like it or not, you're a writer — not a writer who invents and is creative but a writer who reports and is accurate.

Why?

Writing goes with the territory, whether you like it or not. It's a pretty safe bet that you don't like it, but there's nothing to be done about that. A writer you are and writing you must do. If you really think about it the reasons ought to be pretty clear. You write so that everyone concerned will know what you did and why you did it. It's almost frightening to consider how many people outside your department are concerned with what you do. And what you write about what you do must meet the needs of all those concerned people. What you write has to tell judge, jury, prosecution, defense, even banks and insurance companies just exactly what happened as you saw it or as you learned about it from someone else. Each person who reads what you write has to be able to visualize what you saw in the same way that you saw it. When you stop to consider it, you're really being asked to do a tremendous job. As a sidelight of being a good officer you have to learn to be a good writer-reporter. You're a victim of serendipity.

Are you up to it?

You're probably not, but that's nothing to worry about right now. Few officers are. There's no getting away from the fact that police report writing is the least well performed aspect of police work in just about any department you look at, and that police report writing costs more in money and in agony than any other area of police work.

Why should you buck the trend?

The answer is clear. You're part of the new breed, the professional breed. You are the men and women who are educated far beyond the level achieved by the stereotyped officers of the past. The professional demands put upon you are greater than ever before. It's taken a hundred years to change your image from that of bruising hulks with guns and clubs to that of wise and understanding people who are vitally and actively concerned with the society in which we all live and grow. Are you going to blow the whole thing because you can't communicate your actions and your findings to concerned people whose job it is to carry out the processes you initiate with your reports?

No you're not.

This book is designed to help you write what you have to write. The writing process isn't hard, but it is demanding. It has a great advantage, however. Once you master the technique, everything functions automatically. Don't panic. Be calm. Use report writing for what it is: a tool that makes the rest of your job easier.

Chapter 2

Writing Mechanics

By the time you finished the fifth grade you had been exposed to everything you needed to know about the written structure of the English language. If you are a normal human being you have devoted the years since that time to forgetting what you learned. Retribution is in store for you, however, and starting right now you are going to learn the basics all over again. The only good thing about the project in store for you is that now there is a shorter and easier way of getting those basics firmly established in your head.

Why are we going back to those awful fifth grade basics? The reason is simple. If you don't follow the basic standards of clear written communication, the time you spend agonizing about your reports is just so much time wasted.

Of course, if everyone forgets the standards of written English just about as soon as they are learned, why should you bother to fight your way through them again? Once again a simple answer is called for. Just about every profession you can think of demands some kind of written expression. Doctors, lawyers, engineers, business and industrial leaders and administrators all have to communicate something to someone, and it can't always be face to face. That's why writing was invented, and that's why anyone in any profession has to be able to write clearly and directly. You're a cop — or you're going to be one — and that makes you a member of a profession. We're not talking about ditch diggers or baby sitters, janitors or housekeepers. We're talking about professional men and women, people dedicated to protecting and preserving their community. Because you are a professional who will be dealing with other professionals every day in dozens of different ways, you are expected to be able to communicate in a manner that will express your ideas without disgracing yourself or downgrading your fellow officers.

It all boils down to a matter of pride. If you have pride in yourself, in your work, in your field, you will want to express yourself in a way that conveys that pride.

Clear expression is not difficult to achieve, but it does take time to develop the skills that are involved in making yourself and your ideas clear. You can't be a good shot, a good athlete, a good anything without practice, and clear writing demands practice too.

You've already seen the list of people who are going to read your report; just remember that you don't want to disgrace yourself as all those strangers read what you have written.

The Grammar You Have To Know

If you're like most other people, the idea of grammar scares you to death. Don't let it. It's not so bad. It's not so good either, but you want to be a professional, don't you? Well, a professional knows how to use the grammar necessary to express his or her ideas. Actually it's not so bad because you only have to remember a few terms. We can't do without those terms; any other way of talking about them would take up more space than we have available.

The terms you have to know are NOUN, PRONOUN, and VERB. Now don't get upset and run from the room. Remember, a fifth grader knows these words, and you have a lot more going for you than one of them.

A NOUN is simply a name. It can be the name of a person or the title of his job or the name of a place or a thing or a quality or a feeling. Here are some nouns so that you can get back into the swing of recognizing them again after all these years:

George	sergeant	burglar
loving	bookcase	Sharon
Indiana	parakeet	strength
	weapon	

Notice that each of the words on the above list *names* something or someone. You really have to try hard to miss a noun when you bump into one or when you have to use one.

The second term you have to know is PRONOUN. That's just as easy a term as NOUN. A pronoun is simply a word that substitutes for a noun. When you're bored with the noun or tired of using it you simply substitute a pronoun for it. Each word in the following list is a pronoun. Each word, in order, can be used for a substitute for the noun in the earlier list:

    he (substitutes for the person's name)
    it (substitutes for the name of the feeling)
    it (substitutes for the name of the place)
    she (substitutes for the person's rank)
    it (substitutes for the name of the object)
    it (substitutes for the name of the bird)
    it (substitutes for the name of the object)
    he (substitutes for the name of the occupation)
    she (substitutes for the person's name)
    it (substitutes for the name of the quality)

Now that's not so hard, is it? Now you remember what nouns and pronouns are, and you need to know what they are for a very simple reason. You write your report (narrative) in sentences, and every sentence should begin with either a noun or the pronoun substitute you are using for that noun. We're talking here about using nouns and pronouns as subjects of sentences. The subject is the person, place, or thing that the sentence is about. You see, there's really a purpose behind all this. Someone could know all the fine points of grammar and never be able to write a clear report because he didn't know the *form* that report should have. You've just learned the basic form, and you don't have to know any fine points at all. You just keep in mind that every sentence you write should begin with either a noun or a pronoun subject and all will be well.

Of course, there are lots of other ways to write sentences, but they would be designed to accomplish something other than what your report is designed to do. You want to make your reports as clear and as direct as possible, and the easiest way to do that is to shape each sentence according to the simplest and most direct pattern available. In a little while you'll see what the advantages are when you follow the pattern and what the dangers are when you don't.

The last term that you have to know is VERB. Verbs can be confusing; they can cause trouble; but they *MAKE* your report. Master the idea of the verb and you have, for all practical purposes, met the key to the art of writing. A verb is a word that shows some action (shoots, runs, aims, attacks, grabs, speeds) or a word that connects the noun or pronoun to the words that describe that noun or pronoun. Don't panic! It might sound confusing but it's really very simple. Look carefully. The verbs in the following sentences are underlined for easy recognition.

1. The suspect <u>shoots</u> the gun. (*Easy?*)

2. The suspect <u>shot</u> the gun. (*Still easy but now it's in the past tense.*)

3. The victim <u>runs</u> around the corner.

4. The victim <u>ran</u> around the corner.

5. The sergeant <u>is</u> mean and overbearing. (*See how that little verb connects the noun to the words that describe it?*)

6. The captain <u>was</u> in charge. (*No big deal here. That little verb connects the noun to the descriptive words.*)

7. The victim <u>had paid</u> the ransom. (*Very tricky. The verb—the action—takes two words to tell the whole story.*)

8. The victim <u>might have run</u> around the corner. (*It takes three words to express the action here.*)

9. They <u>ran</u> to the suspects. (*Notice the pronoun that starts the sentence. It'a a plain old substitute word for two or more people.*)

10. They <u>were</u> frightened. (*Notice that little past tense verb that connects the pronoun to the description.*)

Now you have your definitions — and some examples — of the three terms you have to hang on to. The definitions are oversimplified. If we wanted to teach you everything about verbs we'd need a hundred or so pages, but the principle is clear and simple enough for you to work with. If you get stuck, consult a standard grammar book or find yourself an English teacher. Both will complicate the issue somewhat, but in an emergency they're good friends to have.

Sentence Patterns in Your Reports

Whatever you write in your report is for somebody else to read. You don't need it for yourself. You recorded what you saw and did, or what somebody else saw and did. Your memory is perfect, so you don't need to write anything down. You'll remember everything about the incident, and when the time comes for you to discuss it you'll be able to reel off all the details in flawless fashion. There's just one little drawback to this comforting picture. Memory doesn't work that way. Most people can't even remember what they had for dinner last night, and when your day, as an officer, is full of incidents there will be times when you won't even be able to remember where you parked your car. You have to write it all down, then, so that the people who need to know what you saw or did or reported will be sure of getting straight information. One of your many functions in writing is to make the reading of that material as painless as possible. To achieve this goal you must follow a certain pattern in your writing, a pattern which has been repeatedly demonstrated as the easiest and fastest way of reading.

This gets us right back to the point of the minimal grammar lesson you have just endured. Start each sentence with the noun or pronoun subject so that the reader will know instantly and without any question just precisely what it is that you are writing about. The easiest way to convince you of the truth of all this is to give you some examples. Read each sentence carefully so that you'll be sure of the intended meaning.

1. After striking the victim, the suspect ran inside the front doorway of the building.
2. In order to meet the entrance specifications, you must pass a vision test.
3. In the intense glare of the flames engulfing the factory, the officer had to cover her eyes with both hands.
4. Dripping blood from four separate gunshot wounds in his left leg, the victim crawled off the sidewalk and rolled under a parked car.
5. Hoping to see the dog on the street, as it was reported to wander the neighborhood frequently, I drove slowly around the block.

Do you understand what each sentence is about? They're not hard sentences. Each one says something understandable *if you read it slowly enough.* In that little matter of reading speed is the whole point and purpose of the proper patterning of your sentences when you write your reports. Not one of the sentences meets the required pattern. Each one is cluttered with introductory elements that block off the noun or pronoun subject so that the reader has to backtrack every time to be sure that he knows what it is that he is reading about.

Look at the examples again. Sentence number 1 puts up a four word block before we get to the noun subject, the thing that the sentence is about.

Sentence number 2 puts up a seven word wall before we get to the pronoun subject. This sentence is about *you,* what *you* must do. The too-quick reader will suddenly go off on a tangent about orders and specifications and miss the whole point of the sentence unless he backtracks and checks the whole thing out again.

Sentence number 3 puts up a ten word block before the reader gets to the officer, the subject of the sentence.

Sentence number 4 delays the reader with eleven words before the victim's actions are revealed.

Sentence number 5 gives the reader seventeen words to plow through before the subject shows up.

The point of all this is simple. Who has time to dig through excess material in order to find out what the sentence is about? The people who have to read your reports, the people who depend on the clear and accurate reporting of your actions are busy people. You're not the only officer on the force. Everyone else is submitting reports, too, and the pile of paper work never lets up for a minute. Simplify your structure so that you simplify the task of the reader. How do you do that? Put your subject first. Look how much more direct, how much more rapidly the point can be understood, when the examples are rewritten to carry out this simple pattern.

1. The suspect struck the victim and then ran inside the front doorway of the building.
2. You must pass a vision test in order to meet the entrance specifications.
3. The officer had to cover her eyes with both hands against the intense glare of the flames engulfing the factory.
4. The victim was bleeding from four separate gunshot wounds in his left leg. He crawled off the sidewalk and rolled under a parked car.
5. I drove slowly around the block looking for the dog which was reported to wander the neighborhood frequently.

You have to admit that you get to the heart of the meaning of each sentence much more quickly this way. A sentence that announces its subject immediately is a sentence that is easy to read. Save your reader's time; he'll be grateful.

This kind of sentence is also easier to *write*. So you see, you're going to reap some benefits, too. It's practically impossible to get confused about where you're going with a sentence if you begin it with its subject. Confusion often results when you try to start a sentence with an introductory word group that gets you sidestepped from the point long before you can manage to establish just what that point is.

Watch Those Pronoun Subjects

It has all seemed easy so far, but just as you would expect, there is a danger point in what you've learned. Those pronouns — substitute words for noun subjects, remember — can cause some problems. You have to remember a fundamental rule about pronouns: they always agree with the nouns they substitute for. If that rule doesn't have too much meaning for you, look at it this way. Both nouns and pronouns can be singular or plural. The rule means that you can use a singular pronoun to substitute for a singular noun. Of course, a plural noun will demand a plural pronoun. In practical application, then, this means that you shouldn't say "it" if you mean "they." Any pronoun irregularity results in confused meaning for the reader. As your goal is to make the reader's job as easy as possible, you want to be sure that you don't fall victim to this kind of carelessness.

Furthermore, each pronoun that you substitute for a noun has to refer to that noun exclusively, not to any other. Usually the pronoun substitute refers to the immediately preceding noun. If it doesn't, all sorts of confusion can result. Let's look at some examples of all this and be sure that we understand the principles involved.

1. The suspect pointed his gun and demanded the victim's wallet. He fled in a green and white van.
   (This says the victim fled. Is that what is meant? Note that the pronoun substitute that leads off the second sentence refers back to the last mentioned person. Can you correct the sentence?)

2. The women called for help. She was bleeding profusely.
   (Who was bleeding? The noun subject in the first sentence is plural, but the pronoun substitute in the second sentence is singular. Do you see the confusion that results when pronouns don't agree with the nouns they substitute for?)

3. The patrol car pursued the speeding truck. They were intercepted at the NE junction.
   (Who was intercepted? This says that both vehicles were. Can the plural pronoun "they" be used to substitute for the singular noun "patrol car"? What did the writer really mean to say?)

4. The victim approached the suspect. He says he was terrified by the gun.
   (Who was terrified? Remember, the pronoun is designed to substitute for the immediately preceding noun. Is this report coming out the way it was intended?)

We grant you that each of the faulty examples shown above *could* be figured out eventually. The intended meaning could be determined in each case. But consider the cost in extra time spent. Do you have the time to probe each and every sentence of a report to be sure that you are getting the intended meaning? Of course not, and your report readers don't have that kind of time either. If you practice enough you can be clear in your reporting. Clear reporting leads to clear reading. We might also point out that if the reporting officer has to be questioned about his intended meaning in a report, then he is only adding to the cost of the already burdensome reporting process.

A Warning About Your Verbs

We said earlier that verbs *make* your report. Verbs are probably the most important words in the language. They carry the meaning of your sentences. They express action, they show connection, they carry the message of the sentence. When we talk about narrative we will discuss the proper choice of verbs, and the reason for that is undoubtedly clear. We want the meaning we express to be as accurate as possible. But there's another point about verbs in your police reports. That point is simply *make your verbs active.* In other words, make your verbs *do* something. Make sure that the person or thing you are reporting about said or did something, and show that action with your verb. Don't say "The railing was struck by the car," but instead say "The car struck the railing." Immediately the report is sharper, clearer, more direct, more *active.*

Police work involves action; it is not a passive operation. Your reports should reflect this attitude. A passive report takes too long to get moving, but an active report gives the reader the situation immediately. Consider these examples:

1. The victim was struck by a green and white van.

(It would be much clearer, much sharper, much more active to write A GREEN AND WHITE VAN STRUCK THE VICTIM.)
2. The shot was fired by Suspect #2.
   (Make that statement stronger and more direct: SUSPECT #2 FIRED THE SHOT.)
3. The child was mauled by the large dog.
   (It is more direct and more to the point to write THE LARGE DOG MAULED THE CHILD.)

You'll notice that in most cases the use of active verbs saves both time and space. Generally you need to use fewer words to report an action in a direct and active way. Passive constructions take longer to write and longer to read.

If you master these simple rules through practice and deliberate effort, you will find that the whole writing process becomes simpler and faster. One of the major difficulties with reporting is that the officer so often feels under some sort of compulsion to dress up his reports. Resist that feeling! A police report is not the place for the creative ebb and flow of majestic or mood inspiring language. You're not writing to entertain or to stimulate your readers. You're not conveying emotion or editorializing on the actions you are reporting. Confine yourself to just what happened. Concentrate on WHO DID WHAT TO WHOM AND WHY.

Using Sentences

This is as good a place as any to hit you again with the idea that has been mentioned earlier:

Write in sentences. Yes, you may abbreviate, and yes, you may simplify, but no, you can't avoid sentences. Start with your noun or pronoun subject; follow that subject immediately with the verb. Narrative writing allows for this approach. Then add anything else that is necessary for clarity. If you try to shortcut this procedure, you're liable to end up with something like this:

Suspect with gun at head.

Now if you have a vivid imagination, that sets up a lot of fanciful possibilities, but if you're trying to explain that cryptic entry some two months later in a courtroom there's a very strong likelihood that that suspect — whatever he was doing — is going to waltz right out of that courtroom ripe and ready to do all over again whatever it was he had done in the first place. It would have taken you no more effort to "sentence" those words:

The suspect stood directly behind the
victim who stated that he felt the
barrel of the gun against the back
of his head.

Yes, it takes more words, but the time saved in blowing the first report winds up in defeating the whole purpose of your job. A moment or two extra spent *now* saves hours of time — and the public — later.

Earlier we said that you may abbreviate and simplify, and if that is acceptable to your department then do so. You may omit articles (a, an, the) where possible and use standard abbreviations. In such a case, the sentence above would now read

"S" stood directly behind "V" who stated

he felt barrel of gun against back of head.

You've abbreviated and simplified, *but you still have a sentence.*

Style in Reports

English majors fret and fume, moan and complain about the assignments they have to write. They not only have to have a decent content, but their grammar and structure must be as near perfect as possible, and they have to have that ineffable quality of style. (If you don't know what *ineffable* means, look it up. You'll probably never use it in a report, but it's a great word to drop at cocktail parties.)

You don't have any of those problems. Everything that those dull English students have to cope with is already solved for you. You don't believe it? Read on.

First of all, consider the matter of content. Content is what a piece of writing is about. You don't have any worries there. That's all taken care of by your job. If you're at a collision scene, your content is what happened at the collision scene. If you're called to a purse snatch scene, your content is what happened at that scene. You don't have to make anything up. You're a writer who has the best of all possible worlds. You don't have to invent anything. With your investigation training behind you, you're a master of writing content.

Second, there is the major problem of grammar. But there's no problem here either. Start with a subject, follow with a verb, then add anything else that is necessary for clarity, and keep your pronouns straight. Composition students go through all kinds of hell trying to vary their sentence form. That will never be your problem. Every sentence you write should follow the same grammatical pattern. You never have to worry about tricky variations.

Finally we come to style. Style has hung up more writers than any other aspect of creativity. Style in writing is like flavor in food. Each reader will respond differently to the ingredients that go to make it up. But you don't have any of those worries. Your style never varies. Your readers will always want their writing flavor served up the same way: direct statement, easy to read and immediately understandable. In other words — are you ready for it, here comes the biggie — *you don't have to be interesting.* (We're talking about your writing here, not your personality.)

Pity the poor writers who have been rejected all their lives because what they write isn't interesting. Weep for the poor tired English comp student who sits over his typewriter night after night working on a report that has all the necessary elements — including blood — but that fails to be interesting. A writer develops interest through unusual content, through careful manipulation of structure and pattern, by creating a flowing and original style that is all his own. If the writer can't create interest in what he writes, his writing is doomed. But you don't ever have to give any thought to those concerns. All you have to do is write down what happened and what you did. Could anyone ask for an easier assignment than that? Your readers are so involved with what you report that they're going to go through it no matter what. You really are what every real writer longs to be, a writer whose readers hang on every word.

Chapter 3

Assembling the Information

You've met the fact that you're going to have to write reports, lots of them. The acceptance didn't come easily, but there's no way to fight it, so a report writer you're going to be. Now is the time for the obvious question: *Where do I begin?* The answer to that comes as a result of all your training; you begin by recording the results of your investigation of the incident.

From the moment you arrive and start absorbing and recording information, your trustiest tool is your pen. You start to make notes of what you saw and what you did as soon as is feasible. Naturally, if you're engaged in a shoot-out or attempting to extricate a collision victim from the wreckage of his car, your two hands are busy. Your mind is at work, however, taking in as much of the scene as you are able to handle so that when the time comes to start getting your actions on paper you haven't forgotten what you were doing there in the first place.

Note-taking is not an overwhelming art, but it is a skill that you will be able to develop with practice. You can take notes in pretty much any form you want *as long as they mean something to you.* Those notes are the basis of the report form you will be expected to fill out, and of the narrative about the incident you will be expected to write, so write clearly and let every word count.

Take pride in your note-taking ability; it is a part of your job. It is best to use a loose-leaf notebook as the keeper of your notes. Match books, backs of old envelopes, or used Kleenex just don't serve the required purpose. Loose-leaf form is best because you're going to rearrange the information you record. You're going to shuffle the material around when it comes time for you to put the recorded information into final form.

Most jurisdictions have a short-cut method of recording notes. Standard report forms are in general use today, and much of the information that you will need to record can be entered immediately on the reporting form. Items such as date, time, type of incident, place, type of vehicle employed, etc., all have their little box to check off or fill out. A representative selection of various types of such forms is included in your teacher's guide. It's an excellent idea to familiarize yourself with the availability of such forms. Who knows, you may be on the next committee to redesign the report form for your jurisdiction.

Short-cut form or not, there is a great deal of information to put down. The only way your superiors are going to know how perceptive you are about police matters is to show them with the excellence and the inclusiveness of your reports, so when you start your note-taking process get everything down that might conceivably be of importance or interest. While one of the things you will learn is how to keep your reports short and precise, it is best to have everything in your notes for possible later reference.

A written document is good courtroom evidence, but even better is the testimony that you will be expected to give. But how do you testify if you don't remember the case? Your notes and/or your investigative report will allow you to refresh your memory. You'll keep so many notes that your personal locker will begin to look like an accumulation point for a Boy Scout paper drive.

Testimony by an officer is a *detailed* account, not a loose, meandering account that we might expect of a non-police witness. You're the professional, and you have records to consult and to convey.

You'll review the case, talk to the prosecutor, and take a look at your original notes before you take the stand. This rule about using notes varies from jurisdiction to jurisdiction, and you'd better be aware of what's expected of you in your case. Common law says that you can use anything you need to refresh your memory. The evidence code of some states is very strictly controlled; this means that any refreshing of your memory must be done from something that you wrote, or personally caused to be written. That means your original notes and/or your full report.

From the time of your first training course up through the months and years to the present you have been taught quite a bit about criminal investigation. One of the key things you learned was that lesson about WHO, WHAT, WHERE, WHEN, HOW, AND WHY — five W's and an H. (That may sound like a rock group, but it's not.) If you don't apply those five W's and an H to your investigation, you aren't going to have the material to write the report. If the report doesn't get written you're going to hear some very loud sounds indeed from your immediate supervisor. Let's go down the usual list of W and H, then take a look at the typical personal description sheet, and apply both of them to any report you have to make.

Questions You Should Ask

1. WHO
   a. discovered the crime?
   b. reported the crime?
   c. saw or heard anything of importance?
   d. had a motive for committing the crime?

e. helped the one committing?
f. committed the crime?
g. associated with the suspect?
h. is associated with or is known to the witness?

PHYSICAL DESCRIPTION
a. Height
b. Weight
c. Nationality
d. Complexion
e. Eyes, color (alert—normal—droopy)
f. Glasses (if any)
g. Visible scars, marks, tattoos
h. Age
i. Hat (if any)
j. Hair, color and cut
k. Beard, moustache, sideburns
l. Shirt
m. Necktie or scarf
n. Jacket/coat
o. Trousers
p. Shoes
q. Weapon; kind and how held

METHOD OF ESCAPE
a. Direction
b. License
c. Vehicle description
d. Additional remarks

2. WHAT:
   a. happened?

b. crime was committed?
c. are the elements of the crime?
d. were the actions of the suspects?
e. do the witnesses know about the case?
f. evidence was obtained?
g. was done with the evidence?
h. tools were employed?
i. weapons were utilized?
j. knowledge, skill, or strength was necessary to commit the crime?
k. means of transportation was used in the commission of the crime?
l. was the motive?
m. was the method of operation?

3. WHERE:
   a. was the crime discovered?
   b. was the crime committed?
   c. were the suspects seen?
   d. were the witnesses during the crime?
   e. was the victim found?
   f. were the tools and weapons obtained?
   g. did the suspect live?
   h. did the victim live?
   i. did the suspect spend his leisure time?
   j. is the suspect now?
   k. is the suspect likely to go?
   l. was the suspect apprehended?

4. WHEN was:
   a. the crime committed?
   b. the crime discovered?
   c. notification received?

    d. police arrival at the scene?
    e. the victim last seen?
    f. the suspect apprehended?

5. HOW:
    a. was the crime committed?
    b. did the suspect get to the scene?
    c. did the suspect get away?
    d. did the suspect get the information necessary to enable him to commit the crime?
    e. was the crime planned?
    f. did the suspect secure the tools and weapons?
    g. were the tools and weapons used?
    h. much damage was done?
    i. much property was stolen?
    j. much knowledge, skill, or strength was necessary to commit the crime?

6. WHY was:
    a. the crime committed?
    b. a particular type of tool used?
    c. the particular method employed?
    d. a witness reluctant to talk to you?
    e. the crime reported?

Naturally, the list is not complete. Every case is different. The list is shown here in this form only as an indication of the type of information you will be recording, because all that information in one form or another will be included in your report. Don't be afraid of making your notes too complete. Several entries from your notes may well be combined into a single sentence in your final report, but you have to have the information to begin with. You'll have ample opportunity to practice note-taking, and combining those notes into a finished report. The main thing to keep in mind at this point is that you should never be at a loss as to where to gather the information that goes into your report. Everything pertinent, including the state of the weather, starts out in your notes and winds up in one form or another in your report.

The standard forms mentioned earlier may, in minor incidents, serve as the core of your notes. A more complicated situation may well necessitate using one of the forms as a scratch sheet along with your notebook. You'll have to see what the particular, individual and always unique situation amounts to before you can decide how it is going to be handled. But in any event have your notebook and clipboard containing sample forms ready at all times.

For example, a minor incident dealing with a resident's complaint about a barking dog will probably not call for pages of notes, or an extensive examination of the scene. But that same resident complaining about a vicious attack by that same dog resulting in extensive biting and bleeding might well demand substantially more material that you must gather.

In your traffic class work you have already learned (or soon will) how extensive your investigation must be, and how every piece of information gathered must be recorded in your notes.

Few officers are able to write their completed reports, even on simple incidents, right on the spot. It may be hours or even several days before you get around to completing your report. You can't trust your memory. You have to depend on your notes to be sure that you are really living up to the expectations of your job.

Separating Fact and Opinion

In your note taking, and in your final report, of course, stick to the facts above all else. The temptation is strong to get away from fact, but hang in there. Don't let your creative impulses take over. Remember that you're not setting out to be a creative writer. You are reporting what happened: who did what to whom and why, not what might have happened, could have happened, should have happened, or didn't happen. Save your creative energies for crime solution. Make your reporting concentrate on facts. Facts make up the backbone of all reports, and *anything other than facts must be labeled as such to avoid any possible confusion.*

So then, what is a fact? The answer is simple. A fact is a statement that can be verified, something that can be known as a certainty. When you are sure of your facts and when you are able to express them clearly, you are in control of the content of your report.

An opinion is a conclusion that you may believe in implicitly, but it can't be verified. There is no way of proving an opinion. You may offer opinion in your report, but don't offer it as a substitute for fact. True, an opinion can come as the result of your interpretation of the facts, but be sure that your facts are clearly stated so that the basis of your conclusion is reasonable.

These two definitions have been expressed in simple terms. They're not legal definitions. It's usually easier to have a clear idea of a term before you start exploring its legal ramifications. You've met these terms before, of course. Have you checked their legal meaning? Remember you are engaged in law enforcement and legality is going to become your middle name.

Black's Law Dictionary (4th edition) has lots of things to say about *fact:* "A thing done; an action performed or an incident transpiring; an event or circumstance; an actual occurrence . . . that which has taken place, not what might or might not have taken place."

The dictionary then goes on to cite specific cases which brought about the establishment of this legal definition, and you can see just what it is that your reports are supposed to be made of.

The same dictionary tells us all about *opinion,* too. "Opinion is evidence of what the witness thinks, believes, or infers in regard to facts in dispute, as distinguished from his personal knowledge of the facts themselves; not admissible except (under certain limitations) in the case of experts."

Once again, the dictionary offers a list of legal citations which established the definition. And once again you can put the simple explanation together with the accepted legal meaning and see what your reports are *not* supposed to be made of.

In the examples we have seen so far, fact has dominated. The location of an accident is a fact, not an opinion. The location can be verified. Facts present no problem, assuming, of course, that your investigative procedures have been accurate and that you have gathered the necessary factual information on which to base your report. Opinions, however, do present a problem, and it is safe to say that as many reports have been bogged down by mislabeled opinion as by faulty vocabulary or style.

Let's look at some examples of both fact and opinion to be sure that we understand the difference.

1. The car was moving at an unsafe rate of speed.
2. The car was moving at 70 MPH.

Sentence #1 offers an opinion. It's not a fact. What is an unsafe rate of speed to one observer might well be reasonable to another. Sentence #2 gives us something concrete to hold on to. Highway speed can be measured. Report the measure and enter the realm of fact.

1. He looked as though he had a gun in his pocket.
2. I saw the outline of a gun in his pocket.

Once again, sentence #1 offers an opinion, but

we have no evidence. Sentence #2 provides that evidence. Assuming that our vision is not faulty and that we recognize the shape of a gun when we see it, we have a verifiable fact.

These examples may seen childish, not worth spending our time on, but this whole area is too important to ignore. The problem is not necessarily that we don't know the difference between fact and opinion, but that we don't report adequately. In each of the preceding pairs of sentences, the first will not result in sure conviction, and the public will be the loser. The second sentence of each pair may well result in putting an offender away for a while. At least law enforcement has a chance to win when the ammunition provided is made up of facts.

When opinion is called for, feel free to give it. But be sure that you tell your reader what it is that you are giving:

It is my opinion, based on the physical evidence reported above, that driver #1 was in fact driving the vehicle which struck and killed the pedestrian.

No one can argue with an opinion that is labeled an opinion. Present your facts, draw your conclusions, and stipulate which is which. When combined with the mechanical skills that you will be learning in this course, fact can be the winner every time.

What Happened When

One of the many things you are expected to be able to do is to separate cause and effect. In other words, the readers of your report need to know the order in which reported events took place. In order to establish the sequence of events you must apply your investigative techniques. It's not much help to write that Car A struck the rear of Car B. It's much more meaningful to be able to write, after your investigation, that Driver A was trying to light a cigarette, lost control of his car, and wound up striking the rear of Car B.

In other words, don't take the lazy officer's way out; show that you're a professional by dealing with the necessary information in a professional way. Don't just write "Suspect intoxicated" but instead state your observations accurately. What evidence of alcoholic consumption was seen? What did the witnesses to the suspect's behavior say? What evidence is there that the suspect, even though intoxicated, could form the specific intent to commit a burglary? Once again, it's the old investigative procedure routine, but that's why you're a professional. There's no point to simply stating a conclusion if you don't offer the evidence to support it.

As mentioned earlier, a representative selection of police reporting forms is contained in the Teacher's Guide. They have been collected from jurisdictions all over the country. The basic idea of all the forms is the same, although there is a lot of individuality in the placement of items and in the arrangement of material.

When these forms were being collected the instruction forms for filling out each were being carefully read, too. It is evident that each jurisdiction provides a detailed explanation to its officers. This text is not going to reproduce those directions. In some instances the instructions run longer than individual chapters of this book. The key factor to keep in mind is that your department provides specific directions for filling out these forms. The goal of each jurisdiction is to make the reporting process as painless as possible. Regrettably the hard part comes after the forms are filled out when you are expected to write your narrative report. This is not to say that the forms themselves don't count; they do, and they count very much indeed. They provide a quick reference to the background of any incident you are reporting, but your ability to combine words in order in the narrative really determines your reporting ability.

Chapter 4

Writing Your Narrative

Most of the writing you are going to be doing will involve *narration*. Don't let the word throw you. It's simply the name of the kind of writing that tells what happened. Ideally, when you narrate what happened you tell the events in their correct order. One of the purposes of your investigative technique is to establish what that order is. We'll look at the problems with that aspect later on, but for now let's concentrate on just exactly what is involved in narrative writing.

First of all, narration is natural. You've been narrating things all your life. Any time you tell what happened you are engaged in narration. Narration is story telling, and the necessity for telling what happened crops up dozens of times every day. When your instructor asks you why your assignment isn't in on time you tell him what happened to prevent it from being done. Did you have a strange dream last night? You're going to tell it to somebody. That's narration too. When you tell what you saw, what you did, what you heard, what you felt, you are narrating because you are telling a story. The desire to tell what happened is universal, so a reporting officer is doing what comes naturally. You don't have to learn *how* to tell, but you do have to learn *how to control* the telling. Gaining that control is not dificult. It just takes a little practice.

Most of your narration is immediately recognizable as such because it is in the past tense. That's understandable. Most police reports deal with something that is over, some action that has been completed. Are you reporting a collision? It happened; it's over. You tell it in the past tense. Are you reporting an interview with a witness? It happened; it's over. You tell it in the past tense.

The tense of a sentence is, of course, controlled by the verbs you use. Good narrative writing concentrates on verb quality as well as verb tense. When we talk about the quality of a verb we are talking both about its literal meaning and its suggested or connotative meaning. This point is a vital one, so pay close attention. Consider these examples:

1. The crowd shifted when the shot was fired.
2. The crowd ran when the shot was fired.
3. The crowd scattered when the shot was fired.

4. The crowd dissolved when the shot was fired.

5. The crowd turned when the shot was fired.

The verb in each of these sentences carries the meaning. All the verbs, in this limited context, might be considered synonymous. But which verb is right? That is, which verb best carries the intended meaning of the reporting officer? Which verb will best express to the reader the meaning that the writer wants to convey? Each verb gives the reader the concept of movement, but each verb also suggests something along with the idea of motion. Look up each of these verbs in a good desk dictionary, and consider the type of movement that each suggests. When you put it all together you're going to discover something very interesting indeed. The verbs that a writer uses tell a good deal about that writer, sometimes more about the writer than about the incident being reported. It's almost impossible to avoid coloring your writing with verbs that suggest your reaction to the action being reported, but as a good officer your goal is to keep that type of response to a minimum.

Here's another way to look at the problem. Your reader is vitally interested in the information you are reporting. Your use of facts and the conclusions you draw from those facts are legitimate and expected parts of your report. But your reader is not interested in language that *hints* and *suggests* more than is intended. In the examples presented earlier, consider what you observed and report it as accurately as possible. If the crowd *broke up* when the shot was fired, say so. Don't tell your reader that the crowd *shifted* (changed formation), or the crowd *ran* (fled in panic), or the crowd *scattered* (went in various directions), or the crowd *dissolved* (vanished), or the crowd *turned* (pivoted). Say what you mean and mean what you say.

In order to accomplish the goal of saying what you mean you have to know what you mean. Here's where we meet a word that you probably hate, but there's no getting away from necessity. You have to have an adequate *vocabulary*. Words are your tools in writing, and any workman has to be the master of his tools. Your vocabulary has to be broad enough to be all inclusive and narrow enough to be exact. That sounds like a near impossible goal, but don't give up yet. In order to control your vocabulary you just have to keep three points in mind.

First, your vocabulary has to be precise. Second, your vocabulary has to be objective. Third, your vocabulary has to be accurate. Let's look at each requirement in order.

Vocabulary Must Be Precise

The need for precision in statements was shown earlier in this chapter in the consideration of verb selection. The differences among the verbs *shifted, ran, scattered, dissolved,* and *turned* may strike you as much too subtle to worry about, but wait until you've hit the courtroom a time or two. When you've had to undergo an extensive examination of just what your words are supposed to mean you'll see the necessity for precision of statement. This matter isn't limited to verbs; any word you write in your report is subject to examination, and woe to the officer who doesn't know exactly what he or she intended to convey. Regrettably, intention is no substitute for achievement. Avoid potential trouble; be as precise and as exact and as specific as you can be. A good rule to follow always is to beware of generalities. A few examples will show you why.

If the witness to a street beating reports that the suspect had a musical instrument in his hand as he attacked the victim, you, the reporting officer, aren't going to get too much mileage out of the account. After all a musical instrument could be a miniature harmonica. However, if your witness reports that the suspect beat the victim about the head with a trumpet we have a potentially deadly weapon to write about. Never mind reporting that a farmer reports the theft of a domestic animal that produces milk for commercial purposes. If a cow was stolen, say so. Of course, it might also be a goat. How is the power of the law going to get the stolen property back if nobody knows what the hell it is that has been taken? In all your writing — subjects, verbs, modifiers — call the proverbial spade a spade. Never mind reporting about a garden implement designed to turn over small quantities of dirt.

So then, precise writing is exact and specific. Avoid the general word and the general statement. Remember the cow, the goat, the trumpet, and the spade. If push comes to shove you can always leave law enforcement and turn to dairy farming, music, and gardening.

Vocabulary Must Be Objective

Objective writing is disciplined, controlled, factual, and direct. It tells it like it is, and no personal feelings or emotions get in the way to color the words. To write objectively is to write what was or what is, *with no personal comment added or implied.*

Subjective writing is much more colorful than objective writing. Subjective means *personal,* and there is no place in police writing for personal consideration.

Consider the difference between these two sentences:

1. He wore blue and green striped slacks, an orange shirt, and a purple scarf that reached down to his knees.
2. He bravely wore loud blue and green striped slacks, a screaming orange shirt that looked so hot it's a wonder his skin wasn't singed off, and a dramatic purple scarf that made a passionate river of royal blood from his neck to his knees.

The first sentence is completely objective; we are told about three articles of clothing that are worn, and no comment of any kind is offered. If the reader wants to form an opinion on the basis of the description, he is at liberty to do so, but the writer makes no comment, offers no hint about his reaction to the sight. The second sentence gives us the same basic information — but with a difference. Now we are offered not only information but also comment — personal comment — subjective comment. The clothes are not only worn but are *bravely* worn; the writer observes the color of the slacks and finds them *loud;* the shirt takes on the dimension of blazing heat; and the scarf now suggests both majesty and intensity. The writer is offering an *opinion* that he wants the reader to share, and to convey that opinion he offers comment along with fact. But your job is not to offer comment. Your job is to offer fact. Chapter 3 stressed that you're not setting out to be a creative writer who needs to offer comment — opinion — on his material. If you concentrate on the factual material you'll have enough to do. Save the comment for the people who are trained to cope with it.

Vocabulary Must Be Accurate

Accuracy and precision are much alike, but where precision deals with the selection of the specific word, accuracy deals with the selection of the correct word. You've been dealing with law enforcement long enough to know the difference between an automatic and a revolver, haven't you? If you mean one, don't say the other. That's what we mean by accuracy of vocabulary. The layman often doesn't know the difference between robbery and burglary or between assault and battery. Selection of the correct term represents accuracy.

Doesn't it seem reasonable that you should say what you mean? Of course it does, but the problem beginning officers often face is that their vocabulary lacks the word choices that should be available to it. How do you expand your vocabulary? The best way is through reading and talking about what you read with other interested officers. We're not suggesting that you are going to be making the obvious errors mentioned in the preceding paragraph, but when you've read as many police reports as we have you would be dazzled by the inaccurate words often chosen by officers who should know better. Our favorite example deals with the case of the decapitated leg. By the time we stopped laughing about that one it was almost too late to urge the officer who wrote the report to undertake a serious course in vocabulary development.

The final point to be stressed in any serious consideration of police narrative writing is, briefly, to be brief. The time to remember that you hate to write is when you are writing. Perhaps then you'll fight the tendency that many of our worst writers have of going on and on and on — and saying nothing. Learn to be concise. How? You learn that by backtracking over what you have written and cutting out every word that isn't serving a useful purpose in your report.

On the other hand, don't overdo the cutting. Being concise doesn't mean that you shouldn't be complete. You must include everything that is needed, and of course that requirement means that you know what is needed. After all, that's what all your police training has been about all this time. You should be able to recognize the elements of the particular crime you are investigating and writing about. Remember, however, that police reports are not supposed to read like a novel. The goal is not to keep your reader in suspense. The District Attorney doesn't want — doesn't need — any surprises. Just eliminate any unnecessary material. What's unnecessary? That's simple. Anything that does not contribute to the clear and accurate understanding of the reader is unnecessary. Remember also the reason for writing the report in the first place. Your report is a record of events. If the record is inaccurate the reader will not understand what you're writing about. If the record is inaccurate the events will not be clearly presented in a courtroom situation. If the record is inaccurate the writer of that record is going to get it in the neck or some other portion of the anatomy.

You're going to spend a lot of time testifying in court. There are few things in life so chilling as trying to explain to a packed courtroom what you *meant* to say. The courtroom is no place to tell of your intentions, but it is a place where your accomplishments will be measured. Don't let them be found wanting.

Narrative Examples

Keeping in mind the necessity for precision, objectivity. accuracy, completeness, and brevity, consider the following example of a part of a narrative report:

Assistant Manager Frank Smith indicated that the safe had been looted and ink spattered over the desk. It was located in the upstairs office which was on wheels. Holes were drilled in the roof to make an entrance next to the utility pole at the back. Footprints on the desk were under holes.

Can you figure out what the reporting officer is saying? Of course not, and nobody in the courtroom would be able to do so either. The officer has the right idea in mind. It's almost possible to see him struggling to meet the requirements of clear communication, but without the skills that reporting demands his case is lost before it starts. Let's consider the various points where the officer failed to communicate:

Sentence 1: Note that verb *indicated.* To indicate means to give a sign. Couldn't Smith talk? Did he just point? If Smith *said* or *stated* something, say so. Next we're told that the safe had been *looted.* That means that the safe had been plundered, pillaged, and everything had been removed, but later on in the report we will find that only the money had been removed from the safe, so why doesn't our officer work for accuracy and say that the safe had been *burglarized?* After all, that's what happened.

Sentence 2: The sentence opens with "It," and the officer meant the safe. But remember that pronouns generally refer to the last mentioned noun, so it would appear that the officer is referring to the desk instead of the safe. Evidently, our common sense tells us, the safe was on wheels, but as the officer writes it the office appears to be on wheels. The mind boggles.

Sentence 3: Was the entrance next to the utility pole? How could it be? A roof is horizontal; a utility pole is vertical. That description "at the back" — does that refer to the back of the roof? How can a roof have a back? Does the officer mean that the entrance was at the back? If so, he should say so, but while he's at it he should also tell us that he means the back of the building, not the roof.

Sentence 4: We've tried very hard to visualize footprints under holes, but we just can't do it. Can you?

Now, let's try to reassemble that report excerpt, this time keeping in mind the requirements of communication.

Assistant Manager Frank Smith stated that the safe located in the upstairs office in the NW corner of the building had been burglarized. A series of connecting 1″ holes had been drilled into the roof making a 14″ x 12″ entry hole to the upstairs office. Access to the roof appears to have been made by climbing a utility pole at the rear of the building. There were footprints on the ink-

spattered desk which was directly under
the entry hole in the ceiling.

Do you see the difference between the two versions? The revision tells us what happened. We are able to concentrate our attention on the crime itself without having to waste our time trying to figure out what the officer intended to say. In the revision we are given the necessary information precisely, objectively, accurately, completely, and briefly. True, the revision takes 30 more words than the garbled version, but it also tells us a lot more. Brevity does not mean incoherence.

We're going to start working on a collision report that was submitted by an officer who really thought he was on top of his job. When his supervisor started reading the narrative, however, the picture he saw was quite different from what the officer intended. Why? Here is what he wrote:

At approximately 2245 arrived at accident
location off US50 where Hopyard Road
comes into it which is a right angled intersection. US50 is a 4 lane highway divided
by shrubbery in a dirt strip approximately
3 feet high. Each side is bonded by asphalt
shoulders. It is 20 feet wide. The highway is
a total of 110 width and travel lane is equal
12 feet concrete surface. Each lane is approximately 8 feet of asphalt shoulder running East-West.

The picture presented by the words you have
just read is unbelievable. Go back and read it

again. It is positively incoherent. Try to visualize just what is being described as the accident location. You say you can figure it out? Well, we can't, but let's assume that you can. Test your mental picture of the scene. Try to recreate the scene in a drawing or a diagram. You'll be surprised at what comes out. Let's see why.

Remember the things that earlier chapters told you to keep in mind — vocabulary, grammar, noun, pronoun, verb, order of events? Now you'll see the reasons. Sentence by sentence is the only way to go. Hang on.

Report: At approximately 2245 arrived at accident location off US50 where Hopyard Road comes into it which is a right angled intersection.

Comment: *Who arrived? Say so by starting with a noun (the officer) or a pronoun (I). Where is the location? If it is off US50, then it must be on Hopyard Road. Or is it in the intersection? We certainly have to be told. And suppose it turns out to be on US50? How will we ever know? According to what is written, Hopyard Road is coming into itself as a right angled intersection. Remember, a pronoun refers to the last named noun, so we'd better abandon the "it" and get the geography right.*

Report: US50 is a 4 lane highway divided by shrubbery in a dirt strip approximately 3 feet high.

Comment: *The hell you say. Are all four lanes going the same direction? Better clarify that. If the highway is divided, where is the division? Is the divider the shrubbery or the dirt strip? And is the dirt strip really 3 feet high? Isn't it the shrubbery that reaches that height?*

Report: Each side is bonded by asphalt shoulders.

Comment: *Be grateful that the sentence is so short; if it were any longer the shock might well kill you. What does "each side" refer to? Each side of what? And whatever it is, are you sure it is bonded? It might be bounded, after we find out what we're talking about, but remember the necessity of having a reasonable vocabulary. Oh, it's a spelling error, is it? Do we have to say anything about that? And how about those shoulders, asphalt or not. Why plural? More than one shoulder is going to make a big difference.*

Report: It is 20 feet wide.

Comment: *What is 20 feet wide? We've been coping with shoulders, and that's a plural word. How can we call shoulders it? Remember, pronouns have to agree in number with the nouns they are substituted for. But do you really mean that the shoulders are 20 feet wide?*

Report: The highway is a total of 110 width and

all travel lane is equal 12 feet concrete surface.

Comment: *110 what? Feet, we assume, but if we add the word "feet" right after the figure, the sentence still doesn't make sense. Is "all travel lane" a meaningful term? If you mean each lane of travel, you'd better say so.*

Report: Each lane is approximately 8 feet of asphalt shoulder running East-West.

Comment: *Impossible, from start to finish. If we interpret it one way, it contradicts the previous sentence; if we read it another way it says that each lane is made up completely of an 8 foot shoulder. That is not what the reporting officer meant.*

Well, what are you going to do with a report that offers such confusion instead of clarity? You're going to do exactly what the reporting officer should have done. You're going to rewrite it, and you're going to keep on rewriting it until it says to the reader just exactly what it says to the writer.

Time for Thought

Before you start trying to straighten out the preceding mess, let's do some serious thinking about the reasons for the lack of clear statement. Does the report indicate that the officer who made it is an incompetent policeman? No, not yet. We may find out later that that is the case, but for now we have a lot of things to consider.

First of all, what does the department expect of the officer? If he has been allowed to "get away with" this kind of reporting in the past, then the blame is not his but the department's. What kind of police department would let such work pass? An overworked one is the most likely answer. With the constant increase in police duties and responsibilities, quite often things that are not quite right manage to slip by. *Sooner or later the problems will be caught,* however. If it's sooner, then the damage can be repaired with a minimum of effort; if it's later, then there's nothing that can be done, and law enforcement has lost its opportunity to carry out its assignment.

Second, was this excerpt we have seen really intended as the final report, or was it merely a combination of preliminary notes and a rough draft of what the final version would be? If the officer is sufficiently rushed, it is quite possible that we have done him an injustice by assuming that this confused version represents what he is capable of doing.

Third, just how serious was the incident that the officer was reporting? If it was a minor affair with no damage, no injuries, and no possible repercussions then *perhaps* we can excuse the officer for his lack of skill and polish in the reporting process. *Of course, we have no guarantee that given a serious incident the officer would be able to do much better.*

So we see that there may be degrees of blame. However, all things being equal, we can't really overlook the lack of expertise that the report excerpt shows. If such reporting style proved to be the habitual pattern of the officer in question, then we would have to say that he was incompetent. We'd have a farewell party for him, wish him well in his new career, and start interviewing for his replacement.

In essence, it's safe to say that a one-time slip in a report probably won't cost you your job, but if such a report should come to represent the standard of your work then you really are in the wrong profession.

If it's any consolation to you, the report excerpt was loaded. No one could make that many errors without really trying. We messed up a good report as an example of all the problems that could be present. Here's your opportunity to show that you're not guilty. We'll reprint each faulty sentence for you to revise in the space provided. Use the comment-clues shown earlier along with your own skills to make the reader see what really happened.

Faulty Version
At approximately 2245 arrived at accident location off US50 where Hopyard Road comes into it which is a right angled intersection.

Your Revision

_____

_____

_____

_____

Faulty Version
US50 is a 4 lane highway divided by shrubbery in a dirt strip approximately 3 feet high.

Your Revision

_____

_____

Faulty Version
Each side is bonded by asphalt shoulders.

Your Revision

_____

_____

Faulty Version
It is 20 feet wide.

Your Revision

_____

_____

Faulty Version
The highway is a total of 110 width and all travel lane is equal 12 feet concrete surface.

Your Revision

_____

_____

_____

Faulty Version
Each lane is approximately 8 feet of asphalt shoulder running East-West.

Your Revision

_____

_____

_____

Now read your whole revised paragraph over. Does it make sense? Does it show what you want it to show? Is there any point where a reader would be forced to ask you what you mean? Try it out on someone else to be sure. Is the location really pinpointed now? Do you see the difference between confusion and clarity?

Incidentally, in its original version this same report included the following lines:

I found the pedestrian's body 32 feet NW of the N side of the intersection in the open field which adjoins the N shoulder. The right leg was decapitated from the body and was located W of the intersection.

Aside from revealing that this was not a minor accident, the excerpt above certainly doesn't add to the general idea of clarity above all, does it? See if you can rephrase those gory details so that the words do the necessary job of reporting. Are you beginning to believe in the need for clear statement of the facts?

Factual information must be conveyed clearly to the reader; that should be obvious. Your training in investigation has taught you that collecting facts is the basis of your work. But mere collecting is not enough; you have to do something with the material. You have to communicate it, and your communication must be clear.

Chapter 5

Make It Real

For years writers of all types have laughed at examples of so-called "federal prose," those gems of confusion that dot government reports and forms. Everyone's favorite example of such writing style can be found in the directions for filling out federal income tax forms, but while the laughter goes on we find that more and more people are trying to emulate that style of writing in their own work. It's the old story of trying to imitate "high class" work, although in this case the high class is definitely misnamed.

The Watergate investigation has tended to highlight this problem as we read and heard government officials saying such things as "This memo is inoperative," and "At this moment in time." Federal prose is easily identified by several characteristics: use three words instead of one wherever possible; use long words instead of short; work for multi-syllable confusion instead of direct communication. It's easy to laugh at examples of poor writing, but when those examples begin to spread and to take over the writing patterns of large groups of writers then we're in serious trouble. Writers of police reports are now helping to spread the disease.

Somehow one doesn't look for police officers to do anything in their writing other than to communicate as directly as they possibly can. Yet over and over again we find that police writing has taken on the qualities of the worst in communication examples rather than the best. The typical police report is almost incomprehensible, not because of grammar and structure (although there are all sorts of problems in those areas) but because of the use of *jargon*, language that is meant to be specialized and technical but which turns out to be meaningless and incoherent.

You have only to read a few typical reports before you begin to fall into the pattern of meaningless confusion that seems to dominate most police writing. It's easy to see how all the bad habits got started, but it's not so easy to see why the confusion is not being corrected on a nation-wide basis. Fortunately, there are some enlightened police jurisdictions that are now concentrating their attention on ridding their reports of the confusion of jargon. Over the next few years we hope all of them will. While we're waiting for that happy day, you should concentrate your attention on trying to avoid the misuse of language. Of course, if your jurisdiction insists on the use of poor style and incoherent structure, then you must follow their policy; however, you're not always going to be in the lower ranks. Eventually you will set policy, and your policy should be clarity above all.

The first thing a reader notices about a typical police report is that nothing ever happens or is reported *directly*. The reporting officer rarely writes, "I saw the suspect throw the knife." Instead the officer has been conditioned to write, "The reporting officer observed the suspect throw the knife." Don't officers ever *see* anything? Why must they always *observe?* It's obvious how this passion for indirection got started: the officer has been indoctrinated with the idea of being and remaining impersonal in his reports. Objectivity is a good thing, as has been stressed earlier. But objectivity is one thing and lack of clarity is another. Prominent law officials, by necessity, have come to realize that the importance of the police report is such that immediate clarity should be the goal, no matter what traditions have to be cast aside. There is no reason to couch everything in third person. The reporting officer should write in first person when he is reporting what he observed and what he did. Study this excerpt from an actual robbery report and see whether or not it is as clear and as direct as you think it should be.

Reporting Officer responded to Jackson

Store 1121 Winsor Avenue this date and time on report of a silent alarm. Reporting Officer contacted on duty clerk Michael Jackson who advised he had just been robbed.

Is the report clear enough for you? Maybe it is , if you have already been brainwashed into the third person nonsense that seems to dominate most police reports. But look at it this way: When this case come to court, is the reporting officer going to refer to himself in the third person? Can you picture the scene in the courtroom:

D.A.—*What did you do when you received the alarm report?*

R.O.—*The reporting officer responded to the alarm. . . .*

D.A.—*Just a minute. Did you write the report? Weren't you the responding officer?*

R.O.—*Yes.*

D.A.—*Then suppose you tell us directly. What did* you *do?*

And that little bit of fanciful dialogue tells why you should report as directly as possible.

Let's take that same report excerpt and turn it into first person direct communication. See what you think of the change.

I responded to Jackson Store 1121 Winsor Avenue this time and date on report of a silent alarm. The on duty clerk Michael Jackson told me he had just been robbed.

Could you ask for anything clearer than that?

Look at how we reduced the length of the

material while at the same time making it more direct. You'll also note that the first sentence correctly shifts to first person. The person writing the report is taking full responsibility for his actions. The minute we read "I did something" we know we're on firm ground. You'll also note that the clerk now correctly *told* his tale instead of *advised* it and that we have dumped *contacted* completely. (Check the *American Heritage Dictionary* on the use of *contact* as a verb. You'll learn something interesting.)

Obviously, everything we have discussed in this chapter so far could apply quite definitely to the material in the earlier chapters of this book, but this need for directness is so important, so urgent, that it deserves a chapter all its own. It is quite probable that some of you will have instructors who will get very upset by our insistence on this kind of immediacy. Old traditions die hard. But the temper of the times is on our side. Change may come slowly, but it does come.

The point of all this is simple: be clear, be immediate, be direct. There is no point in writing "Examination revealed a deficiency in his job-oriented aptitude" if what you mean to say is "He failed the test."

A useful and practical writer is primarily concerned with communicating his point effectively. Effective communication is immediately understandable. It is brief, sharp, to the point. Don't write "It would be preferable under existing circumstances to separate as soon as immediately possible" if what you mean is "Get out." All your writing is designed to convey specific information AS IMMEDIATELY AS POSSIBLE, so don't beat around the bush.

The easiest way of assuring that your points will be made immediately and clearly is to forget all the "traditional" words and expressions that officers have been over-using for years. If somebody *said* something, say so. Never mind *notify, indicate, advise,* and all the other roundabout ways that simply avoid saying what you mean.

How did these traditional words and expressions become so much a part of police reporting? Officers probably were influenced by legal language, or at least by their interpretation of it. But police officers are not lawyers. They're not trained to be and they're not expected to be. The only result of this kind of language is confusion mixed with laughter on the part of the public. Perhaps one of the reasons for the lack of esteem so often felt by the public for police is that police language often doesn't make sense to the people who are the subjects of the reports.

Writing Practice

Re-state the following examples in as clear and direct a fashion as you can. Don't change the basic meaning; just sharpen the language.

1. Every morning and every afternoon the duty officer allows a brief rest period for the purpose of refreshment.
2. The automobile's maximum speed capacity is reached when the speedometer registers 120.
3. The opinion expressed by the majority of the officers indicated that approval of the plan would not be forthcoming.
4. The remuneration, exclusive of gratuities, is small.
5. The film is lacking in those pleasurable qualities that would induce high box-office receipts.
6. Your basic attitudes indicate that separation is the only solution to the difficulty.
7. Officer Johnson's elevation to a higher level of responsibility was accorded widespread public approval.
8. Noxious and troublesome wild growth clutered the fenced area immediately behind the house.
9. The man was suffering from an annoying low-level respiratory infection.
10. The pastry enclosed fruit was kept so long in contact with a high oven temperature that a charred effect resulted.

Revisions are shown on the next page. Check them *after* you've tried to make sense out of the examples.

Revisions

1. The duty officer allows a morning and afternoon coffee break.
2. The car's top speed is 120.
3. The officers rejected the plan.
4. The pay is low.
5. The film is a flop.
6. You're fired.
7. The public approved of Officer Johnson's promotion.
8. The back yard was full of weeds.
9. The man had a cold.
10. The pie burned.

How close were you to catching the real meaning of the over-ripe examples? You see the necessity of direct communication. If you try to write in a flowery style hoping to make an impression, you're doomed to make a bad impression. If carried too far in one direction, writing comes out like a bad advertisement; carried too far in the other direction writing comes out simply incoherent. Strive to be as direct as possible, even to the point of being blunt. We're not suggesting that you move into slang or vulgarity, but only that you have nothing to do with a delicious iced confection swimming in fresh fruit syrup. Call a strawberry sundae by its rightful name.

Chapter 6

Learning To Revise

We hope that the material in the preceding chapters hasn't given you the idea that once the mechanical skills are mastered (or at least are under control) that the finished report will just come flowing out of your pen or typewriter. That kind of luck doesn't happen very often. You'll probably find that you have one thing in common with all other types of writers, and that is the necessity to revise your work. Revision is more than just re-writing; it is the sharpening and the shaping of your material into a finished product that meets the goals established for it. You know what your goals are, and you know for whom you are preparing your report. With a little experience under your belt you will know how the readers of your report are going to respond to what you have written.

Every reaction you get to what you write, from sergeant up to judge, should contribute to the whole learning process. In time, you will be able to anticipate questions and objections, and at that point you will be a finished report writer. (That means *accomplished,* not *exhausted.*)

You already know enough about the reporting process to make a fair start on the revision of a faulty report. The example you're going to be working on for a while is not as extreme as the report in Chapter 4. We'll present a short section of the report with comments about problem areas. See if you can recognize the problems before we point them out to you.

Report: Responded to Solano store on report of silent alarm. Just held up by WM wearing paper bag over head and simulating weapon for clerk on duty Jones $25 lost.

Comment: *Who responded? What was held up? Was the money lost or was this the loss in the hold-up?*

Report: Clerk Jones described S as 16-18 years old, 5-10, 150, freckles with brown eyes underneath. Rounded shoulders in blue overalls. S ran WB on Solano Ave. away from store. Radioed other units and search made.

Comment: *Is that description clear? Radioed what information? Search made where?*

That's enough for now. Consider the report and the comments carefully, and revise until you have a good, clear, direct, and active report (excerpt). Keep in mind the things you have learned so far. Here is a reminder:

1. Full sentences.
2. Sentence pattern.
3. Noun (or pronoun) subject at start of each sentence.
4. Specific details as needed.
5. Clear verb use.
6. Exactness of expression.

With these points in mind, you should be able to straighten out the above report. You may have to invent a piece or two of information, but that's legitimate for practice purposes. Discuss your revision with other officers or trainees to be sure that you are saying what you mean. When you're satisfied that what you have written really says what you mean and what you need, then compare the original and revised versions again. As further practice, you ought to be able to discuss the step by step procedure that you went through in order to bring that report excerpt up to professional standards.

Here is a full narrative summary report that is almost very good. It needs some revision, some tightening, some attention to the previously listed reminders. Read it carefully and see how you can improve it. (A list of generally used abbreviations appears at the end of this chapter for your use.)

Narrative Summary

Comp advised R/O at the above location this date & time he was driving his veh

N/B in the 2400 blk of Chestnut. The above listed veh passed the comp on the R/H side going N/B then pulled susp veh IFO comp forcing comp to stop. Susp #1 exited his veh at this point and ran towards comp. Upon reaching comp veh Susp 1 (the driver of the susp veh) reached inside comp's veh (driver side) and unlocked the driver's door. After Susp 1 opened the driver's door he grabbed the comp by his throat. At this point Susp 1 called for Susp 2 to give him a hand. Susp 2 grabbed comp by his legs and held him down. Somehow comp got one leg free and kicked susp 2 in the face. Susp 1 held comp in a strangle hold in the back seat of comp's veh. Susp 2 then proceeded to go through comp's pants pockets and wallet. R/O observed comp's L/R pants pocket torn half off. Loss was located in comp's front left pants pocket. After Susp 2 found the money in comp's pocket he (Susp 2) removed comp's keys from ignition and opened the glove box. Susp then proceeded to go through the glove box contents. Susp 1 advised Susp 2 to go and look in the trunk for a handgun. Susp 2 could not open the trunk. Susp 1 let the comp free and ran in an unknown direction. Susp 2 followed.

Susp 1 lives in Oak Tree Project. Comp knows Susps 1 and 2. Not their address. Susp 1 has a sister that lives near 10th and Pine and should be there if not at home. R/O went to Oak Tree Project but found no matching veh. Comp can ID both susps. He further advises R/O both Susps hang out at 10th and Pine daily.

That report is really pretty good, although some experts would prefer to have all abbreviations eliminated. The officer has made a strong effort to be accurate and complete. He's avoided jargon (abbreviations don't count) and has tried to be clear and direct. However, some revision is called for. For example, the verb choice is not always ideal. The officer refers to himself in the third person. The sentence structure and pattern is not flawless, and the statement about the sister is not at all clear. See how you would go about revising the report. Be prepared to explain every change that you make.

Here is a more complete report of an off-beat incident. See if it does everything you (the critical reader) want a report to do. The report opens with a listing of evidence followed by the narrative summary.

Evidence:

(1) Cash: One hundred and seven dollars found in rt frt pocket of Susp #2 by Smith 1234P–turned in to Prop by 1234P.
4-twenties; 2-tens; 7-ones = $107.

(2) Cash: Sixty seven dollars found by 1234P in Susp #1 rt frt pants pocket - turned in to Prop by 1234P.
3-twenties; 1-five; 2-ones = $67.

(3) Prophylactics, "Trojans" rubber–red box container three rolled w/ 1234P/5678P

marked on box. Comp was given them by Susp #1 & #2. Comp gave them to 5678P. Turned in to Prop by 1234P.

(4) Yellow card — Smith & Jones Bail Bond Agency, 999 - 9th St. 1234P & 5678P marked on back. Given to Comp by Susps 1 & 2, Comp gave card to 5678P. Turned in to Prop by 1234P.

Loss:

$142. 2-tens; 2-ones; 6-twenties = $142.

Narrative:

At approx 1300 hrs, 1 May 76, comp was walking into a restaurant at 2nd and Main when she was approached by Susp #1 who stated his name was Buck & that he wanted to have some coffee w/Comp. Comp said no, but Susp #1 followed Comp into restaurant & sat at table with Comp. Susp #1 started discussing his pimping activity & wanted Comp to work for him. Susp #2 then sat down at table and said his name was Mac. Comp attempted to leave but Susps #1 & #2 told her to stay. Susp #1 grabbed Comp's purse and took above loss from purse. Susps #1 & #2 then took Comp via bus to apartment at 2029 Main where Susps #1 & #2 made Comp remove her clothes & wear the clothes supplied by Susps #1 & #2. While there Susps #1 & #2 instructed Comp on how to obtain tricks & what prices to charge. Susps #1 & #2 gave Comp above evidence #4 & told her to use it if Comp got busted. Susps #1 & #2 also gave Comp Evid. #3. Susps #1 & #2 drove Comp to motel at corner 3rd and Walnut at approx 2300 hrs to pick her up after Comp had about three tricks. Comp called police at approx 0030 hrs 2 May 76 and Comp explained above to R/O 1234P. R/O's waited at 3rd and Walnut with Comp who noticed veh N/B on Walnut from 3rd at approx 0115 hrs w/Susps #1 & #2 inside. R/O's stopped veh. Comp positively I.D Susps #1 & #2. Susps #1 & #2 arrested for Kidnapping, Robbery, Pandering.

Are you satisfied with that report? We'll admit that it's the best one we've shown yet, but there are still some things about it that need revision. Consider it carefully. Determine what needs to be done and then do it. (Hint: It's not just the structure and wording that need some revision. There are also some specific duties that we need to be told about. Put on your investigative hat as well as your revision hat for this one.)

These examples and the practice you're getting in the revision process are not just busy work. Generally the hardest thing for any kind of writer to learn is the necessity for revising what is written. You may sometimes find it necessary to revise the same report three or four times until it really says what you mean. The important thing to remember is that revision time is not wasted time. You have to keep in mind at all times the specific audience you're writing for. Can the prosecuter build his case on what you have written down? You're not a lawyer so you can't be dead certain, but you can give him better than a fighting chance. As you re-read what you have written you must examine each word critically. Is it direct, is it clear, is it precise? Don't ever be satisfied with a report that does less than meet that goal.

When you had a report or a paper to write back in your old high school days, do you remember how you used to die a little bit until you got the assignment finished? You were generally so glad to get something — anything — down on paper that the idea of revising, of correcting, of throwing out useless material was the last thought you had. Fill up the paper and get it in was the goal. Well, those days are gone forever. The writer who doesn't revise deserves what he gets, and he generally gets some very unpleasant experiences as a result of his failure to do his job.

The greatest writers in the world spend more time revising their work than they do creating it in the first place. You should do no less; in fact, you should do more. The demands and the expectations put on you are higher than they are for any other kind of writer. Your reports show that you have done your job and that you recognize your responsibilities to the community you serve and help to build. Remember good old Officer Johnson in Chapter 1.

Abbreviations That Are Common in Police Report Writing

ADW Assault with a Deadly Weapon
AKA Also known as
A/O Arresting Officer
Arr. Arrest
Att. Attempt
CID Criminal Investigation Div.
Comp. Complainant
Def. Defendant
DMV Dept. of Motor Vehicles
DOA Dead on Arrival
DOB Date of Birth
E/B Eastbound
F.C. Field Contact Report
GOA Gone on Arrival
HBD Has Been Drinking
H&S Health and Safety Code
IFO In front of
IRO In rear of
L/F Left front
Lic. License
L/R Left rear
N/B Northbound
NFD No further description
NIP Not in possession
NMN No middle name
P.C. Penal Code
PIN Police Information Network
R/F Right front
R/O Reporting Officer
R/P Reporting Person

R/R	Right Rear
S/B	Southbound
S/C	Suspicious Circumstances
S/N	Serial Number
Susp.	Suspect (Some jurisdictions use S)
V.C.	Vehicle Code
Vic.	Victim (Some jurisdictions use V)
VIN	Vehicle Identification Number
W/B	Westbound
W&I	Welfare and Institutions Code
Wit.	Witness
YSD	Youth Services Division

Chapter 7

Writing Description

So far all the materials and examples we have dealt with have involved the writing of narration. After all, the narrative report (or narrative summary) is usually the major part of your writing work. But there are other types of writing you'll have to do as part of your completed report. Probably the most frequent added writing involves description.

As a general rule, we don't have to worry too much about writing a physical description of an individual. Most departments have a printed form that covers such physical descriptions. You fill out clearly labeled boxes that cover such points as height, weight, complexion, hair and eye color, etc. Several of the sample forms in the Teacher's Guide show examples of how to give a physical description of an individual. But it is a description of another sort that we're concerned with here, and that is the description of *things,* things that are stolen or things that are found, things that are somehow or other involved in the case that you are investigating and writing about.

The idea of such description doesn't seem difficult, but it puts very special demands upon any reporting officer. For example, when it is necessary for you to describe articles of clothing you're going to find that you're expected to have a lot of knowledge that you have never given much thought to before. You have to know styles and fabrics, and, of course, you have to know enough about fashion to ask the victim or the witness the right questions. It's not going to do much good to report the loss of a woman's blue coat, but it's going to be very helpful to report the loss of:

Woman's coat, light blue wool, full length, Princess style flared from waist, dress type.
Black dyed Persian lamb collar and cuffs.
Dark blue silk lining. Size 10. Value $225.
See the difference?

Here are some points to keep in mind about the description of clothing. You'd better do some extensive practice to be sure you can handle the material.

Clothing: Give the name of article to be described. Always indicate size, color, maker's label, laundry or cleaner's marks, kind of material, and value.

Examples:

MEN'S SUITS: State whether double or single breasted; whether two or three piece (coat, vest, and pants; or coat and two pairs of pants); whether evening, street or sport suit; state kind of lining if any.

MEN'S COATS: State whether overcoat, short jacket, raincoat, single or double breasted; type of trimming, lining, whether or not belted.

WOMEN'S SUITS: State type of suit (sport, dress, tailored); number of pieces; color and type of lining; color and kind of buttons; type of trimming.

WOMEN'S DRESSES: State type (evening, street, house); style; kind of trimming if any (lace, fur, contrasting, self-trim).

WOMEN'S COATS: State whether full length or short; flared or straight; evening, sport, or dress type. Full description of trimming, buttons, etc. Show color and kind of lining. For fur coats state kind of fur, style, lining, etc.

See all the things you have to know about? The point of knowing is not just to be able to write the description but also to be able to recognize the items when and if you see them.

There are all sorts of other items you have to be able to describe and recognize. Here are additional listings of the many subjects you're going to have to become aware of.

Jewelry: After giving name and value of the ar-

ticle to be described, include the following whenever it is a logical part of the description:
1. Color and kind of metal.
2. Number, kind, color, and size of stones.
3. Type of mounting (filagree, plain, engraved, etc.)
4. Type of setting (basket, tiffany, sunken, etc.)
5. Inscriptions, dates engravings, initials, serial numbers, jeweler's markings.

Examples:

BRACELETS: Give width: whether link, filagree, solid, flexible, or half-clasp type; whether plain, engraved, or stone set. State if safety chain is attached and type of clasp.

BROOCHES AND PINS: Give size and shape: whether plain, engraved, or filagree; also whether pin has safety clasp.

BUCKLES AND MISCELLANEOUS: Show size, color, shape, stones, etc.

EARRINGS: State style, length; whether screw, clasp, or pierced type; color of stones, etc.

EMBLEMS, CHARMS, ETC.: Show size, shape, name of lodge or club (Elks, Masons, Sigma Chi, etc.)

NECKLACES: Give length, number of strands; whether matched or graduated stones or beads; whether strung on thread or chain (give color and kind); describe clasp.

PENDANTS: Show size, shape, strung on chain, ribbon, cord, or thread; give color and type; describe clasp.

RINGS: State kind of metal; kind and number of stones; whether plain, engraved, or filagree; any inscriptions or initials.

WATCHES: State make (Bulova, Hamilton, etc.); movement, case, jewel number, size, type of case, whether plain, engraved, or set with stones. If it has a chain or wrist band attached, describe color, material, length, etc.

NOTE: If any of the preceding are matched sets (earrings, necklace, bracelet, etc.) so state. Also, if you are unable to write a clear description, include a small drawing of the item.

Household Articles: Give the exact name of the article being described. Always give number of articles, color, size, maker's label, serial numbers, or other marks and value.

Examples:

BEDDING: Sheets, pillowcases, blankets, spreads, quilts, etc. State what the article is. Then give a complete description of size, color, material, cleaner or laundry marks, monograms, etc.

FURNITURE: State what the article is. Then give complete description stating what kind of wood or metal, color, kind of material covering, and trimming. In cases of matched sets (bedroom, living room, dining room), give number of pieces in set and state the number of pieces stolen.

LAMPS: State kind — floor, bridge, table. Give kind of wood or metal of the standard. List the number of globes, whether it is a reflector type, if it has a base light, and color, size, and description of the shade. For table lamps, state whether the base is statuary, glass, china, pottery, or metal.

PIANOS: Show maker's label and serial number, if any. State if upright, spinet, baby grand, grand, concert grand.

RADIOS AND TELEVISIONS: Show maker's label, serial number, model number, number of tubes; whether console, table, portable, low- or high-boy type; size of screen, etc. Give kind of wood or metal; show color and kind of trim if any.

RUGS: Give size; color or combination of colors; whether plain or design; domestic or oriental; type (Broadloom, Axminster, etc.); maker's name when known; cleaner's marks; whether fringed or bordered; stains, tears, marks, etc.

Other Kinds of Property: Give name of article to be described. On all articles listed, always show the maker's or brand name, serial and model numbers, size, color, and value. Show any initials or other marks of identification that have been added after purchase of articles.

Examples:

AUTOMOBILE SUPPLIES AND EQUIPMENT (other than tires): Spotlights, wheels, trunks, tubes, carburetors, spark plugs, etc. Give size, color, maker's name, serial numbers, number of articles, and other marks of identification.

BICYCLES: Give name, size, kind of seat, brake, tires, baskets, horns, lights, etc. Indicate color and serial number if known.

BOOKS: Give name of book, publisher's name, author's name, color and kind of material binding, approximate size of book, any written inscriptions, book plate, etc.

BUILDING EQUIPMENT: Includes lath, wire, plaster, bricks, stucco, glass, marble, lumber, roofing material, paint, nails, cement, etc. Give size, color, number or amount of articles, any serial numbers available.

CAMERA EQUIPMENT: Give maker's name, model number, serial number, lens number and name, shutter number and film size. State type of camera (movie, box, single lens reflex, etc.). State kind of material of camera, projector, case, etc.

CASH REGISTERS, TYPEWRITERS, OFFICE EQUIPMENT: Give maker's name, size, model, serial number, color, etc.

DOCTORS' INSTRUMENTS: Includes stethescopes, blood testing apparatus, hypo needle outfits, etc. Give maker's name, size, color, etc. Show case size and color.

DRUGS: Give amount, kind, any other information available.

ELECTRICAL EQUIPMENT: Toasters, irons, generators, motors, etc. Give size, color, model and serial numbers, wattage, voltage, maker's name, any other marks or inscriptions.

GUNS: Show maker's name, caliber or gauge,

color of metal, serial numbers, type of handle or stock, marks, inscriptions, initials, etc. State whether revolver, automatic pistol, rifle, or shotgun. If shotgun, give number of barrels. Also show any holster, cartridge belt, etc.

There are lots of other kinds of materials, but there isn't time or space to include them all. You ought to have the idea by now of the kind of information to include. Basically, you use common sense in providing the clearest and most complete description you can.

Where do you learn all the information that you have to include in your descriptions of things? That's an easy question. The answer is in two parts. Part One: Your personal observation. Part Two: Take a long close look at a standard catalog, such as the Sears' catalog or Ward's catalog. Look at the illustrations and then read the accompanying descriptions, ignoring the excess words that are intended as a sales pitch.

Faulty Example: Covered vegetable dish. Styled to perfection with secure fitting cover to retain heat and flavor. Practical and pretty. $8.95.

Revised: Covered vegetable dish. Stainless steel. Maker KROMEX stamped on bottom. Two piece: dish and cover. 10 x 3½″. Value $9.00.

You're going to need a lot of practice writing descriptions, and the best way to get it is to as-

sign yourself some definite projects. If you can't think of any for yourself, try the following. Check your result out with other class members and with your instructor.
1. Describe the flatware (silver service) used in your home.
2. Describe your television set.
3. Describe your watch.
4. Describe a matched set of books from your own collection or from the local library.
5. Describe three different outfits (clothing) of your own. (Make the writing useful—skip the jeans and T-Shirt).

We haven't said anything about the major item that is stolen every day—the automobile. Every department that we have dealt with has a report form for auto theft, and labeled spaces are provided for make, year, model, color, etc.

Chapter 8

Taking Statements

Your work in investigation has shown you the necessity for taking statements from witnesses, complainants, and suspects. It's not always possible to write a strong and effective report by merely summarizing the comments and remarks of such individuals. When a specific statement is called for, you have to get it and write it down. It's not always feasible or even desirable to haul someone into the station house to dictate a statement to a stenographer or to a tape recorder. There's no need for complicating things unduly.

A statement is the literal reproduction of the actual words spoken by the individual. But often statements instead of clarifying the situation only confuse it. You've already discovered for yourself the simple fact that people ramble when they talk. Most people aren't trained in logical thought and expression, and as a result when they are called upon to tell it like it happened they wind up drifting all around the subject and rarely if ever get right down to the point in a clear and helpful fashion. It is your responsibility to help the person overcome that natural tendency. In other words, you are going to have to teach the person whose words you want to copy down exactly the same things that you have learned in your report writing course so far.

Wait a minute; don't panic now. We don't mean that you have to engage in a classroom situation and teach the fundamentals of grammar and sentence structure. But you do have the responsibility of holding the person you're interviewing to the subject at hand. In essence, you have to be a creative listener, and when you hear the subject being abandoned for a side issue or when the order of happenings gets distorted in the telling you have to bring the speaker back to the subject by questions that are skillfully phrased and politely asked.

It's not necessary to worry about cleaning up the speaker's language. If he uses "street talk," record it as he says it, but hold him to the subject.

You'll find that most people, even when they're not suspects in a crime situation, develop a kind of fear or panic when they are talking to an officer. Psychologists tell us that this fear is induced by contact with an authority figure (that's you) or by the simple fact that most people think that they have something to hide (such as that stop light they ran last week); but whatever the cause, it does happen. You have to be firm but patient when you're taking a statement. Sometimes it's a slow process.

Generally, the best way to go about it is to have the person tell his story to you in his own way. Just listen; don't write anything down. Let him use this telling as a rehearsal. When he has finished, try and tell the story back to him. Don't distort his meaning in any way. Use his words where possible but omit any side issues that he may have included. Then take out your notebook and ask him to tell it again, slowly enough that you can get it all down. Of course, if you have a tape recorder, things are that much easier.

The statement taking process could possibly go something like this:

COMPLAINANT: Well, I was walking down this street, you know, and all of a sudden out of nowhere it seems this guy walks up and grabs me by the arm. Well, that was one hell of a surprise, you know, 'cause I ain't never seen this dude before and he whips out this knife and says to give him my wallet and watch. Well, hell, I ain't going to argue with a rough looking dude like him so I says O.K. What the hell else you think I'm going to do with a knife in my gut so I gives it to him and off he runs, you know, and then I sees you in your black and white and waves you over, you know, and that's what happened.

YOU: Fine. Now I understand. Let me be sure I've got it right in my mind. Now, you were walking down — it was Powell Street, wasn't it — between Post and Sutter on the west side of the street was it? — and this was about lunch time? That's twelve o'clock is it? —

Do you see what you have to do? You let him lead the way, but you pick up the missing pieces along the way. Don't jump down his throat, tell him he's not being helpful, start using TV cop talk about being accosted and observing things and all that garbage that's as far from real as it can be. You're taking his statement because for one reason or another you need his statement. Don't frighten him off and make him sorry that he called for you in the first place. There's a little matter of public relations present here in addition to the facts of the crime. Don't ever forget that so far as the public is concerned, you are the police department. No matter how busy you are, no matter how long it may take for you to get the story told clearly, you stay there and be supportive and encouraging. You're dealing with your public. They pay you.

Another kind of problem is present when there are several witnesses to an event. You've undoubtedly already discovered for yourself that no matter how little a person saw he still feels duty bound to contradict what somebody else has to say about it. Here is where your self control, your patience, is really needed. Don't let the witnesses hassle among themselves. It takes only a few moments for an assertive speaker to convince a whole flock of people that they saw what he says they saw — even if they didn't. Take the witnesses one at a time, and do what you can to keep the others from comparing and contrasting and ultimately distorting the whole story.

It never does any harm to keep reminding the people involved that they're helping the situation when they talk to you. Lots of people seem to have a fear of "getting involved," whatever that happens to mean to them, but nevertheless they all like to feel that they're doing some good for themselves.

Practicing statement taking is not easy. You and your fellow officers are conditioned to heading directly to the point, so setting up a practice situation is rather a problem. But perhaps you can employ some of the exercises from your observation work. It's always amazing to learn that different people see the same action in different ways. You and your fellow officers or your instructor may want to set up an incident and demonstrate how a variety of witnesses have a variety of responses to a single stimulus. Perhaps just being reminded of the difficulty involved in making a clear and precise statement will be enough to induce in you a patience and resignation that will better prepare you for the field work you're going to be doing every day.

There is, however, an interesting assignment that you all can do. Agree among yourselves that on a certain night you all will watch a particular crime show on television. You'll be watching separately, in the privacy of your own quarters, so there won't be any "outside" influences to lead you astray. Prepare an interview that you as the reporting officer would conduct with the major character (obviously not the chief cop in the show). You will all have seen the same show, so you'll all be reporting on similar facts. Write out a statement that you get from your skillful questioning — imaginary questioning — of that character. It would be helpful if you also showed what questions — clever questions — you asked to lead that character to a precise telling. Comparing your individual results at your next meeting will be very revealing. In fact, the whole process can be so helpful that it might be safe to say that at last there is a use for some of those idiotic television programs that we all seem to watch in spite of ourselves.

Chapter 9

Some Encouraging Words

Well, you've done it. You've made it to the last chapter, and you're entitled to a pat on the back and the promise of a future pension. But what is it that you're being congratulated for? What have you accomplished as you worked your way up to this point? Don't reach for it; we'll tell you.

You've learned to apply the principles of clear communication to the part of your job that you dislike the most — writing your reports. You haven't learned *how* to write reports; you knew that before you started, but you have learned how to *revise* and *clarify* your reports so that they do the job they are designed to accomplish.

Never forget that your reports start the whole criminal justice system. They make their way up the ladder from you to the D.A. Clear reports keep the D.A. off the Chief's back, the Chief off the Captain's ear, the Captain off the Lieutenant, the Lieutenant off the Sergeant . . . and when everyone is happy that keeps them from dropping everything on the low man of the totem pole — you.

Now that alone should be reward enough, but there are even more plus factors in store. If your report is correct the first time, then you don't have to re-write and re-write and re-write. While your friends are sitting in the good old squad room working on their reports, you're going to be off duty, getting to bed early, engaging in your favorite pastime. You have instant status: you play while they work. Of course, you worked hard to learn your reporting lessons, but let your friends think that you're just naturally brilliant.

The knowledge that you are doing your total job well gives a lot of satisfaction and makes you more aware of your personal worth. When you receive compliments on your reports from other cops, from supervisors, or in open court from the D.A. and the judge, then you'll know that it's all been worth while. Did you ever think that you would be praised for your writing ability? Get ready to hear it; you've earned it.

Somewhere around the start of this book you recognized that your objective presentation in writing is as much a part of your police duties as helping old ladies across the street or chasing armed robbers. Maybe back then you even remembered the last raking over the coals you earned when a report didn't properly cover the elements of the offense, or when you failed to identify the perpetrator and connect him to the crime scene with good associative evidence. That kind of embarrassment should be gone forever.

We're not suggesting that your newly good, clearly written reports will secure convictions automatically. In the first place, not every case is going to go to court. Conviction and acquittal, guilt and innocence are not for you to determine. But that top notch report you whipped out is going to bolster the prosecution. The D.A. is no fool; he's going to court when the state has a case worth prosecuting. If he feels that your report is going to be vital to the prosecution, then your job has been well done.

Further, your clear report will help to clear up some of the delays in our court system. With your clear report opposing him the accused may well cop a plea on advice of counsel. Plea bargaining is a fact of legal life, but your report can make it easier for the D.A. to fight for a good bargain rather than a poor one.

Clear reports are often the basis for the case being submitted directly to the judge — no testimony, no examination, no courtroom drama. The judge takes the case "on the report" at the request of both sides. Because your report is clear, precise, complete, and intelligent both sides will accept it on its merits.

What else is going for you now that you're an aware report writer? Better crime reporting, good relationships between and among agencies, reduction of certain types of crimes, and, most important, improved public relations and public support can all be brought about because you know enough to make your writing do the job it's supposed to do. Good reporting also means better opportunities for advancement and quite possibly higher salaries.

Crime reporting is important to you, really important. The F.B.I. doesn't accumulate all those crime statistics just to give their computers something to eat. Everything has a purpose.

The report of a crime has to start with an incident brought to your attention. Either you see it happen or some citizen tells you about it. The first case presents no problems: if you see something happen, you'll take some enforcement action. The second case is sometimes a problem; not all offenses are reported. If the citizen feels nothing will come of his report of a crime, meaning he won't see any results, there isn't much point in griping to a cop.

But the citizenry does have an awareness that we sometimes tend to overlook. If they feel that their reasonable complaint will get fair attention, will be investigated and reported, and that the criminal justice system is concerned with giving them satisfaction, then they are going to be cooperative with you. Remember, you are the whole system to the public. They don't get much contact with probation, parole, corrections, district attorneys, judges, and all the rest of the people that make up the system.

A good cop does something about everything that's brought to police attention. And you're a good cop or you wouldn't be reading a book designed to help you improve your reporting skills.

Crime reports are based on the incidents that are brought to the attention of the police and *properly reported.* The spot maps in your squad room materialize because you got the information, you made the investigation, and you reported the results of that investigation. You're a pretty important part of the whole process, aren't you? Isn't that report as important as the officer who made it?

We're not being naive about all this. You're not going to eliminate crime. But you can help to cut it down. How? By eliminating the opportunity through prosecutions that come about *directly* from your reports. Of course, prevention isn't nearly as exciting as action. But the kind of action you often have to engage in is, in brief, hazardous to your health. While the department really does go all out on the funeral, you won't be around to enjoy it. How much wiser to prevent criminal opportunity through clear reports that secure prosecutions that lead to convictions.

Look at it from the other side if you don't quite trust the virtues we've just extolled. When the crime rate goes up and the conviction rate goes down, who gets blamed? You do, not the D.A., not the judge, not the jury. The system starts and ends with you. Without you and your report writing skills there just isn't too much need for anybody else.

So then—if you think you've wasted time learning to sharpen your writing skills, think again. When every cop can do his full job—and writing is part of that job—there's going to be a fine new day around here. Let the whole process begin with you.